Self–Storage

Self–Storage

poems

Rebecca Hoogs

Stephen F. Austin State University Press
Nacogdoches ★ Texas

STEPHEN F. AUSTIN STATE UNIVERSITY PRESS
PO Box 13007, SFA Station
Nacogdoches, TX 75962
sfapress@sfasu.edu
936-468-1078

For information about special discounts for bulk purchases, please contact Texas
A&M University Press Consortium, sharon-mills@tamu.edu or 800.826.8911

Manufactured in the United States of America

LIBRARY OF CONGRESS IN PUBLICATION DATA
Hoogs, Rebecca
Self-Storage / Rebecca Hoogs. — 1st ed.
p. cm.
ISBN: 978-1-62288-015-7
I. Title

CONTENTS

One

Two

Three

For Larry

One

This Myth

This myth is about a girl lounging naked—
just another day in the glade—waiting
for her fifteen minutes of transformation.

In this myth, there is a special inhibition;
men plant marigolds at highest noon
and not one wilts again and again. This myth

features whippets and an unnoticed rabbit perching
above them on a strangely sturdy flower.
Ok, now hold it. This is the moment of holding it

for what feels like forever. In this myth, Time
spaces on his date with Truth and she is always
never letting him forget it. Her face is unfinished

of tears. *(You write about your personal mythology,*
he said, greatly offending me. So I turned him into a tree
and cut him down and have been using him

as firewood ever since.) At the moment, this myth
could be any myth. In this myth, I hire some babies
to dress the place up with garlands. For a price,

they will also exterminate dragons. In this myth,
I live in a birdcage painted with foolish peacocks,
starlings, swallows and other emotions

too numerous to name.

What For?

after Yannis Ritsos

You wouldn't want me, anyway,
always making the world less mysterious.
Always insisting on the city limits.
Did you know *here is the body*
dissolved to *hoax*? Did you know *mystery*

means *I shut my mouth and close my eyes*?
You've seen the longing of captions
to capture the photograph. You've seen
the tour group leader's sadness, flagging
in front, ever alone. Always I know
where I'm going.

So what is the use of maps,
of seeing the sights, of handbooks
of our commonly used phrases,
of certainty, of *of*?

I had lost my subject: two saplings
baffled by wind. Such little saps,

sweet on each other.

Another Plot Cliché

My dear, you are the high-speed car chase, and I,
I am the sheet of glass being carefully carried
across the street by two employees
of a plate glass company, two generic men
who have parked on the wrong side
of the street because the plot demands
that they make the perilous journey across traffic.
And so they are cursing as rehearsed
as they angle me into the street, acting as if
they intend to get me to the department store, as if
I will ever take my place as the display window, ever clear
the way for a special exhibit at Christmas, or be Windexed
once a day, or even late at night, be pressed against
by a couple who can't make it back to his place,
and so they angle me into the street, a bright lure,
a provocative claim, their teaser, and indeed
you can't resist my arguments, fatally flawed
though they are, so you come careening to but
and rebut, you come careening, you being
both cars, both chaser and chased, both good
and bad, both done up with bullets
that haven't yet done you in.

I know I'm done for:
there's only one street on this set
and you've got a stubborn streak a mile long.
I can smell the smoke already. No matter, I'd rather shatter
than be looked through all day. So come careening; I know
you have other clichés to hammer home:
women with groceries to send spilling, canals
to leap as the bridge is rising.

And me? I'm so through.
I've got a thousand places to be.

L'Oeuf

The *zero* has an eggy form,
and so in French, they call it *l'oeuf*,
which is *love* to our oafish ears.
We mishear love all over—
multiply it like loaf to loaves,
like fish to fishes.

Me, I've seen lots of l'oeuf—
then none. Some miracle
that was. I was left
with a small omelette,
with l'oeuf on my face,
a little yolk on my sleeve,
my shell. I'm broke—
a Humpty lover.

Love is a brunch, a racket.
I know it means nothing,
barely worth the oofing
before the offing, but still
I load up my basket
and watch them hatch:
chicklets of zip.
Good l'oeuf!
we're fluff birds.
Gag, oof—
we're tweetless cheeps.

Wishes

To start: a lot of money; lots of lots—
some oceanfront, some not; then, a wide

high-wire, loud applause, and the sweet spot
shining, a sequin flashing both bright sides;

not to fall, to be fallen *for*; a meteor
to sell to fools; to not have eaten

those six seeds, that love grenade, that evermore;
for evermore good whiskey and a good chase scene;

for bang-up jobs; for a vase from a verified era;
for everything in mint condition;

that if I seem to be drifting, you'll be where;
that if I turn to moonshine, I'm drunk;

that you'll *See Below* my heart, that asterisk.
To end: no end, of course: another wish.

Honeymoon

Suppose you know your friends
    have been together for five years
        without ever having sex, and then

they marry, even the words *we're enjoying*
    the toaster seem scorched onto the thank-you note,
        seem frenzied with innuendo.

And there they are, up against
    the kitchen counter of your mind,
        the settings twisted to dark,

burnt bread panting out hotly from the two slots
    like twin beds aflame, a jar of something sweet
        tipped and spilling a slow motion stream

to the tile. Perhaps it is not how you would do it,
    but it makes sense, how they did it:
        the wedding in the Midwest,

the land like a sheet, one corn-colored mile
    unfolding after another. The honeymooning
        not in Greece or *Paree*

but at home, all things being new
    and sharp as untried registry knives.
        Imagine the bear

standing before that at-long-last hive,
    how he's all skin and bones
        from living so long

on just nuts and berries.
   Listen for the bees of *yes*
    and *no* and *not yet*
swarming sleepy, subdued from the smoke
   of the fire just lit. Above, the hunger
     moon grows to overflowing.

And the first taste—
     the condensed collection, the work,
       the wait, the intricate dance

of all those years—
     tastes sweeter taken straight
      from the paw.

Suck

Sucker, suck-up, suck-face,
sucker-punch, this sucks we say,
meaning *it's bad, you're bad,*
bad, bad, bad, not meaning
the cups
and hooks
of the paper nautilus;
or the pull of water in the wake
of a ship; or a sup,
excellent tipple, indeed; or the breast-pocket
where criminals tuck
their guilty hearts;
or a lollipop, suckabob,
all-day sweet; or a ploughshare
applying itself to the ground;
or the perfect disks
of snail-fishes; or the succumb
of air after the blast
in the mine; or a partial vacuum;
or any extraction of any kind
such as honey
from flowers or blood from body
or you
from me;
or the small stalk
of the Roman lettuce;
or a runner taking off
from the strawberry; or the very young
rabbit; or making out like mad in an alley;
or the rising-valve of a pump;
or a punch
without warning, a pain
I wasn't expecting;

or any derivation,
such as comfort or meaning;
or to draw in, draw into, unto, until;
or to inhale, to exhaust;
or me, a creature
of in and out,
of dependence, of attachment;
so what
other option but
to be a sucker? So, it sucks
to be me. I suck.

Miss Scarlet

She's tired of all the accusations,
all the whodunit, with what, and where.
So there's no Mr. Scarlet to call honey bun,
so she wears red, so she *might* be a whore,

but she's certainly not a murderer.
If there's anything to confess, it's that
she fell hard for Plum. He used a word,
weapon without a playing piece, to shatter

her heart. In the billiards room. Now all
she wants is to ditch this mansion,
get a pied-a-terre, a church to solve
her sins, and a little mother-of-pearl gun

more delicate than that revolver. Shit,
the question should be: who *hasn't* done it?

The Short List

I *am* concerned about it; about loss
of its habitat, its genetic pool, about nets
and soda-can rings and poaching, about whatever
in its river, about toxic mold in its walls, of its eventual
need for girdles, about it being whistled at, about its seep,
about it being in my neighborhood next week,
of how to deduct my taxes for it, of sulfites,
of cracks when it heats and cools, of what's carved
into its bark, about it growing, about it staying,
about it going, about the test, the word, about the cookie
afterwards, of its rainforests and the song birds that shade it,
of it slipping across the border, of its airbag embrace,
of its up-and-at 'em, about meeting its eye, about dust
in its lungs, of too much of it too late at night,
of a letter from it, of its chicken little into my lap, of its light,
of its tick towards me, of the thin wax covering it,
of its fading x-ray vision, of its silence, of its dark,
of its smallpox of the page, of too little of it too late at night,
of its ability to get a job or even move out of the house,
of its ever after, of its never before, about the right glass
to drink it from, about the right fork to eat it with,
about the right cycle to wash it on, about whether or not
to check yes for it, about how to answer when it calls
and asks me if it can have a minute of my time.

Pseudomorph

I feel like a me-
like shape, like the real she

has cast me off, spurt me out
and left me to face her predators,

like the real me is off
enjoying her airpocketless body,

while I stay behind going blotto,
a so-so blurb on the back of a book,

a blurry word. My beak keens
for something to say, but I'm a bubble

that's lost its thought, an ink-tank
without a think. O morph, o nym,

I'm know I'm just your pseudo,
your thin skin, but please

return my heart and other vitals.
It's thankless, this being *like*,

this being not quite right.

Self-Storage

"Little soul little stray / little drifter / now where will you stay / all pale and all alone / after the way / you used to make fun of things."

                                                       —Hadrian, trans. W.S. Merwin

It's unreal the way I keep returning to places
like this one, distant from where I live

and in ruins, yet where I live. In my brain,
there is a picture I took of you, picnicking

in the canopis before I caved. Such thoughts
are scattered among various collections

both public and private. In the So-Called
Gymnasium, concrete and rebar crocodiles

are modeled upon ones once marble
which were modeled upon ones once flesh.

Above (my head here, your head
neither here nor there) a dome

mimics the idea of a hairdryer in an idea
of a beauty salon. So I wanted to look pretty for you,

so what? (Some years later, sitting in a coffee shop,
a fire truck named HEAVY RESCUE tore by

but did nothing to pluck from my chest
what had crushed me falling from the viaduct.)

It's all too real how I keep myself
to myself. I have rented a self-storage unit

on the edge of a natural depression. I am
the stuff I store. So sky, keep your bolts
to yourself. If you don't have sunshine to say,
say nothing at all. Look at the way this place

tells us almost nothing about Hadrian
and even less about Egypt which he loved

because it had killed his love. Look at
this fine example of compartmentalization:

paper wasps making a living in the mouth
of a crocodile, twice removed.

Pie Hole

Volcano to which I throw virgins virgins virgins
in hopes I won't say something I shouldn't.
Box of little bones with which I polish other little bones.
Cave close to my brain, hide-out for tongue,
that snail in shell, my petite escargot
which I baste in words I may or may not say.
Some are curious, venture out; some are wallflowers.
Some statements have lived in my mouth for years.
Hole to other holes, foyer to my body's other sad stories,
O mouth, let's elope and explode. Let's run off together.

Instructions to an Operative

Forget that you saw me here, or drew
me near. Forget this morning,

the pass on the park bench, the pat-downs.
Give this glass of wine to your giant;

he'll unwind while I slip by. By-and-by,
the ink I'm written in will cease even

to be invisible. Forget what went down,
the briefcase, its might, what may have been

in it for us. We've had our last secret handshake.
So, get on; anchors aweigh. I'm spelling you

from this intelligence. I'm missing you
from this mission.

Autobiography of Silence

I was the swinging door giving thanks. I admitted your garbage
was mine. I was a plastic poinsettia in July.
I auditioned for the role of an almost empty auditorium.
I was the pane of glass troubled by a rock.
I was the hands the man clasped behind his back to approximate
     contemplation.
Here I am as a Japanese woman and Japanese mountain. Both of
     us in profile.
I am my sister's brother.
Both girls on a bench with flowers fat and skinny,
     stemmy and heavy-headed.
If one is not careful one will fall through the floor rotted
     away from the rain.
If one is not careful one will fall through a bad memory.
The Moscow restaurant where the old couple wasn't talking; he was
     smoking and   looking past her; she was looking down,
     wishing something to look at would be   invented.
I was the unlit twin sconces above them.
Also the desk with the head on it.
And the pillow's savage nap.
My sister's brother's wife with a pouf of wedding springing from
     her forehead like a   Greek   god.
I divorced the interior from the exterior. I wore a headscarf to keep
     my dreams neatly   together.
I was your wallpaper and always autumn. This was at the
     Metropolitan Museum of Art,   circa 1983.
Bored couples sat on the feet of my columns in the Vatican.
I was that pink stuffed panda.
The desk in the sea at Crete.
Seven daffodils and two Russian pensioners.
It seems that I was the dance hall always waiting and sadly it seems
     the bigger the   corsage the less I was asked. I spoke roses, but
     no one came.

Commute

The evening's amber alert lights up.
Modern sunset, another abduction,

and fuck, traffic is bad. The girl
in the next lane texts while driving,

her mouth like the knotted pucker
of a helium balloon. Everything electric blows

eventually: lightbulbs, crushes, what have you.
Even *dynamite* has fizzled to mean *super*.

Annually, too many people at a party
crowd a lanai and it gives way the way

one day collapses on top of the next.
This summer's disaster is coming up.

I commute but am not moved. *That jerk.*
Sometimes I touch a nerve to see if it still works.

Woodwinds

First chair, first clarinet—I had no choice
but to lead a section of uglies.

The blonds all played the flute, silver
tips in a hollow-boned flutter at the feeder.

I kept my mouth against the reed,
the lick of wood, the bamboo buzz.

And while they perfected the head tilt
trill—the purse and kiss—we plowed

through Sousa's oompas. His bams.
While they begged the question

with blue-eyed octaves, we followed
the anchor into the murk, poured

the cement, pulled the shade.
Listener, you must remember

the ring in your bones, the engine
running in the garage, the heat

your hands made. I wonder what
you clapped for? Shells and feathers, light

on the ground, or cables stringing house
to house, green glass broken in compost?

Open House

I may not look it, but
I'm fabulous inside.
Gutted to my gut feeling,
I'm bride-new for you.
I've got good bones,
but am zoned

without you. I'm staged
for life. I've got a mother-in-law
but no husband, a master bath
but no ever-after.
My poor curb-appeal aside,
I'm virtually turn-key.

Come, carry me across me.

Come Here

When, in a sprawling subterranean housewares shop
of Rome, I asked the price of some wine glasses,
and the salesman told me and then told me
to *veni qui, come here,* I went.
He showed me some other glasses.
Do you like these? he asked. I don't speak
much Italian so said only, *sì, mi piace,*
yes, I like. Crystale, he said, and pinged the glass
with a fingernail. *Yes,* I repeated, *crystale.*
And then he touched my arm saying *veni qui,*
veni qui, and so we went to another part
of the breakable underworld where real
about-to-be-married Italians were filling
their bridal registry and so like me
did not yet have all their words for negativity
and he stopped before another set of glasses
and said, *you like?* And again, *yes, I liked.*
And again he rang the tiny bell of what he was
trying to sell me. And then, arm touch, come here,
and then yes, I like. This went on for some time
until I'd liked it all. I liked and was like every glass
he held. All I was was touched. All I could say was *yes*
to everything but bought just two small glasses
from which you and I have yet to drink.

Undoing

They say we're compelled
to erase *a* from *asymmetrical*,

to lop *lop-sided*, to even out *uneven*.
But isn't aberration relief?

The solar eclipse a beauty mark
on the sky's otherwise moony face?

The tremble in an orbit a reprieve
from the rotary disclosing

the same machines? Planets
wander more than thought.

When you returned, I was
happier not having

expected you back.

Song from the Antarctic

The day you were to be saved
dawns at sixty below. The sky

is iced over. You are left
to finger the hot spot in your breast,

the place where the cancer taps its ash.
Above this wildfire, your hand

is a slow satellite, each finger
an expert on you. Of second opinions,

you have ten. Of a way out, none
for now. You have x-rays

of a marriage, cracks
threaded blue, biopsies

and test tubes. Perhaps it was
something you swallowed: a baby

tooth, snow pinched to a pea,
one of the pushpins from the map

of all the places you'd been. Maybe
you gave the cancer something

to work with, work around, and it rubbed
its twigs together, sparked a fire

to race across your tundra
to thaw the earth you thought too bare,

too cold, to burn ever again.

European Vacation

A shirtless man in a skiff in the mid-day sun
waiting to row tourists to the Christ of the Abyss;

Christ subsurface wearing a wave-worn face;
Church bells appealing for Sunday; Sunday holding out;

beach chairs praying for their return to the fold;
children tipping each other from boats;

screams ringing off the harbor walls,
arresting siesta; old woman echoing the lovely once,

sunning the two large tears of her breasts;
divers, all who dive, emerging blessed.

And us? Dry. Just holding our breath.

After after Song

Would a hedge be a hedge
without its inner edge?
Does a thought
inherently contain
an ought? For a long
time I was young,
then I was not. At heart
there's half a laugh,
and in the half-hearted,
even less than that.
This particular ticker
is bird-brained, in-bred,
a little too much come hither
crossed with dither.
The thing is the thing
can't hear itself think.
It's a dumb beeper
always paging me
with its bleeping
emergencies.
Give it a rest,
give it an inch, an ear
and it will take it greedily
just to hear itself beat: *na na*
na na na na
hey hey hey
Goodbye.

Villa D'Este

Water and stone get so ordered around
it's hard for them to break the mold

of *fountain* or *spout*. I can't imagine
another life for them. And the shrubs, too,

are pruned within an inch of their collective life.
Only the blackberries over the garden wall

are having a field day. They prepare
their semi-real berries for impermanent birds

or drop them casually as names. A lifetime ago
there was an ice cream stand here

that's not here today. *Tell me*, the vendor said,
impatient. What did we want

sometime in this lifetime? We settled
for ice cream sandwiches and had them

sitting in the pea gravel. Today I look out
on thunder that would scare an emperor

and tell you (a different you) about my minor surgery.
I would tell any you almost anything

just to have someone to tell you to.
I am gushing, yet clipped, living within

an inch of my life.

Two

A Long Spell

1.

Begin with observation and comment,
then proceed to question
and misdirection. Gesture
toward narrative, as if uncaring.

You are an exchange student
doing a home-stay in staying.
Your host mother is divorced, practices
alternative medicine. Once a week she leads
a group of adults in singing.

She says you have a beautiful voice.

Remember to come to a resolution of sorts,
but never a little epiphany.

2.

For example,
bees foam at the mouth
of the hive like bullets
just before being caught in the teeth
of the great conjurer Chung Ling Soo,
born the very non-Chinese William Robinson.
Both he and his guise died of this trick.
Something's happened. Lower the curtain,

they gasped, feeling the bullet
pull the faster fast one
on their chest.

They were also the first to shoot a girl
from a cannon.

This is the role bees would choose, liking
the *smoking from the hole,*
the *beautiful assistants.*

3.

For example,
in the hayfield, round bales
are bound in white plastic like downed clouds.
Sun keeps pushing its pretty rhetoric
from the sky's soapbox
while the trees let it drop.

Never have we been so divided,
me on this coast,
you on that.

4.

For example,
Napoleon's horse, Marengo, survived
his master by eight years. A snuffbox
was made from his hoof.

It's hard to know what to do with this.
Some details are recalcitrant,
resist pulling the chariot.
I'm terrible
with plot, with action, with making
anything happen.
May I offer you
watermelon, chrysanthemum, fireworks
silkscreened on a fan?

May I offer you a still
of the hoof dreaming in tobacco?

5.

For example,
saying the cup goes with the saucer
doesn't make it so.

Let's not save ourselves
for good but be for everyday.

Hear them rattle each other?

Let's be small stones
engaged in a calculus.
Let's be must-haves.
You be clavicle and I touch.
Just this once, let's be
of mythological proportions,
the best words in the best order,
fumbling for the other's buttons.

6.

For example,
in the race for the periodic table,
elements were found,
but doubted,
unfound.

The promise of snow
isn't snow.
Years later, the lucky ones
were rediscovered,
renamed.

Let me be lost, then your find,
yours to dub, your sudden,
century storm.

7.

For example,
before an electron collapses
to a point in space and time,
it could be anywhere—

The research on uncertainty is boundless.
There is nothing
not being studied.

(Full disclosure: I am married
to the subject.)

8.

For example,
on the sidewalk, a leaf-shaped stain,
a blueprint of decay. Saints don't,
so we bring in the butcher.
The relic business is a good one.

I've seen St. Catherine's head and Galileo's profane finger pointing.
I've seen the souvenir sellers of St. Peter's square.
I've seen the fortune tellers of Piazza Navona. All they ask
are palms.
I've been torn
apart, and apparently am still
on a tear.

9.

For example,
an illusion: "Marvelous Without Skill."
The thought is a circlet of paste pearls.

We go around and around:
Does the road lead in or out of the city?
They say he walked it on his way to the cross.

We forget that a fig is a flower turned on itself,
We forget the weight of paving stones
and adore the mint growing earnestly between them.

We live a life of perpetual astonishment,
lit cigarettes appearing consecutively
and continually.

10.

For example,
how bad is it to be feather-brained?
The cranium fledged with lofty ideas,
the think tank plumed for flight,
notion making its nest,
whirlybirding the skull.

What's worst is the feather-said.

Some birds are scolders.
Some say their own names
over and over.

11.

For example,
at night, lights like nerves
seem all that's left of skyscrapers,
like an alternate ending,
that's lost when
sun sweeps up.

We knew what would happen;
the trailer comes before.

We'll never get made,
so lie with me
on the cutting room floor.

12.

For example,
the Eiffel never gets a break
so I'll give her the vanish—

lull her skyline's story, another gap
in this manuscript of absence.

Please look where I look:
observe my most convincing tricks with sugar,
my best fluttery knucklers. Observe me driving you
to distraction.

And *voilà*, she's gone, as lost
as Mozart's body was on the way
to the grave, the blizzard
too dense for his followers
to follow.

(I was looking at you.)

But that was untrue.

13.

For example,
after me, the flood,
Madame de Pompadour supposedly said,
a sort of *carpe diem*, big living
after big hair.

I, too, have been

too seized by the day,
too much the oar,
that dabbler in cold,

that swizzle stick
of ornamental lakes.

I've gone so far,
I'm no longer oar, nor boat,

I'm landscape and weather.
No court favorite,
I, Flood.

Three

Id *In Utero*

Because there's so little time,
I begin with the d's, where my name is—
or what they call me for now, Delilah—
a joke, ha-ha, and find I'm defined as delicate,
but also a harlot, a temptress! I'm destined
to betray the man I will love and that hurts me,
for I'm sensitive, or I *think* I'm sensitive.
Like roe, I haven't got a thick skin yet.
I'm still a little see-through, not much
more than a deposit, a bit of dirt
at the mouth of a river. But soon
I'll go down it. I'll surface and hitch a ride
on a riverboat to Delphi. I'll ditch the dolphins
and this delphinium of a womb.
I'll be delivered and decide for myself:
doldrums or delight? delirium or dell?
I'll be a person who deliberates,
but I won't be a demi-anything anymore,
and even though they'll give me a new name,
one they deem more suited to an innocent,
Delilah will be deep-rooted, I can see.
A bad deal? Perhaps—but then, that's me.

Heart, My Box of Snow

made it to Florida.
And then I went for a walk.
The frog pond is half iced over.
I chucked a stick at it:
still thin.
On the white side,
the wind twirled a leaf around
like a prepubescent figure-skater
who's given up her childhood
to get here. Of course, the leaf
was wearing its practice costume
of browns, the whole world
offed of spangles as I am
offed of you. Why
mail snow?
Just to show
I could keep it cold
in so much heat.

Dear Diver

—after the Tomb of the Diver, Paestum, Italy

I'm here at the Beach Athena
but the *A* has fallen away. I've stolen
no floaties from no children
and the sun has given me
many compliments. Once in a while
there is a Greek noise from the loudspeaker
and a mother digs a hole and buries her child
up to his knees. So you'll see
it's still mythological here
thousand years after you.

We visited your ruins yesterday.
I hate to tell you this, but it's a hot mess.
On the up side, you are beautifully reproduced
and everywhere. You're in fine form,
a perfect score.

As for me, I speak a simple version of myself,
one without much past and little future.
I know best how to talk about myself,
and a bit about you, whoever you were.
The third person does not interest me.

Diver, I wish you were here, wish
you were not so under the weather
and earth and ether and everything other.
I wish you were not so over. Wish
I could be here thousands of years
from now, like you, little dangler, little hanger-
on, going after the afterlife
like a knife goes after

your cantaloupe,

Rebecca

Ariadne on Naxos

It was a Wednesday

when you left me

shuttered in siesta,

surveying my site

of dreams, dread

a drop of sweat

just about to bead

my back. Was it hot

in the high-noon,

hauling our hearth-stone

through silent streets?

You left a scarab

in its place. Please,

ply me with lies.

Tell me in thread

that thugs drugged you,

gods graved you,

satyrs agreed

you should spend your days

sweet-talking spines

from their heels. Then let me cut

my long-lining

for the possessive case,

the personal pronoun.

This island life isn't

so bad: iced tea,

afternoons afloat,

art films, and fêtes.

Soon, I'll say yes

to a slick-suited grape

god. We'll grope,

groan, grow old.

I'll forget

our go, the gild

of bull's blood

away from Crete.

have been, a butcher's

life, a nice nine-

But soon you'll see the sea

its debts to the ocean floor;

cry from me,

So lie and lie

I'll survive this shipwreck

on your hands as we burned

(Your wife, you know, I would

bride. A nice

to-five for newlyweds.)

take sides and settle

you'll be a far

the maze, amour.

low, love.

and more.

Three States

1. LABORATORY

We're studying mind over matter—
a glass of half full, half shatter.

You're the control group,
your brain a bouquet of some nerve.
That time you made up a word
you were off the charts.

2. BEACH

But a beach isn't life. We're doing some crazy paving
with our bodies, and the sun paves us back, and I'm craving

the spotlight but also the not-light. Half a word
is often enough, scientists say, to indicate the thing.

How about half a heart?
Watch out: gets hot enough thoughts burn off.
Dew-like. You-like.

3. PUBLIC SQUARE

The sun is a cutout, ragged-rayed. A hack job.

The fallout is fountain. Words are an angry mob:
little stones being thrown.
Even the statues have their hearts arrowed
out. Even the birds are just paper targets
from the shooting range: one-note

Nellies, one-hit
wonders.

Lion's Teeth

When others more decorous
are bent on composing, crafting
the trousseau (a thousand hands
preparing petals, another thousand
embroidering spores), I admire the indecent
burst of the dandelion, the straight-up
bloom so soon after snows.

Well before the cocktail hour,
she is freshly dressed, her cheeks
pollen-powdered, her feet squeezed
into the well-broken earth. And when others
are just showing an after-dinner blush
(a tendril just beginning its unpinnings)
she's waving her Fourth-of-July,
baring her lion's teeth.

True, she flashes her underside white
to the wind sooner than might be proper,
but she does enjoy the music.
And true, she might go to seed
before the night is through, but
I admire what becomes of her:
bald bones, milk-sweet spine.

When others hold back their burst
allowing only one white petal
to show from under the shawl, I can't help
but wish that I too could seduce
that solo from the sun. A dizzy dance
out back. Can't help but watch her steps,
listen as she calls to him:
Faster,
Hotter.

Misunderstanding

Around the ruins' reflecting pool,
the caryatids have nothing to stand for—
no lintels or beliefs to shoulder—
and so in the evenings they drink aperitifs,
play mah-jongg with tiles

made of the extremities of men.
They gossip in gibberish and reminisce
about the perfume bottle they saw once
in an Etruscan shop: a woman's head,

full of scent. Always, they regret
thinking better of it. But the talk
always turns and the limoncello,

goes to their unstoppered heads,
and then fumes beyond

like deflocked canaries,
loosened moons.

A Vestal Virgin Holds Her Breath, Counts to Ten

One flame to tend again and again;
time burns both ends.

Two constellations in a square
each dealing solitaire.

Three hazelnuts—two blanks.
Your life? Like that: one blink.

Four ways for wind to blow by day,
but at night there's hell to pay.

Five points to arguments and stars;
hold out your heart for Mars.

Six figs, like questions, fall from the tree;
how sweet a third degree.

Seven decanters, seven nights.
Sleep pours like whiskey, neat.

Eight clothespins, arrows, streams.
Eight flaws in marble weep.

Nine angels at nine looms; at noon,
they nap in wooden spoons.

Ten wishes charged by chariot.
The question: fade or flare?

Daphne In *As the World Turns*

Before all that hot pursuit,
I lived a pastoral existence:
meadows and mead and suitors swimsuited…
But Apollo? Blacklisted.

In the end, I died a pastoral existence,
or wish I had, anyway.
Apollo—black tempered, incensed—
turned pirate, barged up my waterways.

What wishes I had were waked away;
he had a fast boat.
I turned on the waterworks,
turned on my heel, wrote my footnotes,

but he had a fast boast.
I got to shore, got treed.
He's such a heel. Footnote:
I'm turned, gone bad.

I'm got, for sure. I'm tree
in meadow, see? We're completely unsuited.
But I'd do it again—the turning, the going—
not for what ensued, but for the ensuing.

Grenade

Little garnet thrown from the hand,
little heart grown on a sleeve,
like a grain of the pomegranate,
you've got a grip, you're a loaded word
about to blow. Persephone

would say that the pomegranate
is only an apple livid with seeds—
then, how dark down there (She and Eve
compare their field notes: genus, species
a botany of botched affairs).

In dreams, seeing this flesh fruit
ranges in meaning the way *red* can range
from *live girls* to *long life*. But there's no telling
what you mean, dear grenade, no easy denotation,
so the dreamer's on her own

as the besieger—a handsome devil—
breaches, and you're in her hands now.
No matter what she chooses to do,
all you'll do is tell (a thousand tiny bells
toll) and tell (a thousand ruby cells

explode) and tell. All there is
is telling, and then
is told.

Shelley's Jaw

A piece of bone holed up in a jam jar
thinks he's not half the jaw
he used to be. His woe's an old saw,
he knows—aging, death, blah blah blah—
but still, he'd like to *say* so, blab
it in metered syllabics, ad lib
an epic tale of his end—sun, storm, jib
giving way. He also has to admit
he'd like to say he's sorry to whatever bits
of Keats exist to hear it (a pretty ringlet,
probably). And his first wife—Harriet?—
he's sorry to her, too. He didn't really carry
his weight, there, what with Mary
being so much more nubile…but mostly
he'd like to write a poem for his ghost,
and express the gist
of his existence: the great
poet, once bigger than God,
now smaller than a breadbox,
and deader. But it's effing
ineffable, being relegated
to this reliquary, and he's got
a long shelf life to go.

Rus in Urbe

In those days, boxwoods formed a ragged labyrinth
around dry fountain mouths—fresh out of big ideas,

stumped for small talk; wild fields wooed the walls
of the ordered; three children were caught mid-toss,

a green ball in the air. There was a long spell
of time where nothing touched the ground.

Really, it had all gotten pretty boring—all the rise,
all the aspiring. We were waiting for it to fall

like Rome. In the meantime, we remembered
our days spent burning marble, stacking statues

like cordwood, that time we accidentally let the labyrinth
go to hell. In the meantime, we resolved the heated conflict

of milk and coffee and looked forward to the one time
a year we knew we could watch the ball drop.

Descent

A wolf-pack of birds
does a U-ie in the sky.

So, too, do words.
Buxom meant *pliant*,

astonished was once
struck by thunder.

Each day I see farther
into the forest,

the effects of the storm.
Some trees are astonished.

Others are bent, nearly
mean their reverse,

the way a young woman
becomes my grandmother,

now archaic only.

Self-portrait as Porcupine

Out walking, the dog
darts off into the woods,
comes back barbed
as St. Sebastian came back
riddled by arrows.
The key, this time,
is unspinning:
arrows re-quiver,
the saint unsaints,
the dog is unhurt in reverse.
Even language
dumbs down, and you
go back the way
you came, know less
and less with every step,
as snow snaps back
to the sky and the stream
retracts its debacle.

You really let yourself go,
settle into a waddle,
and all your quills,
all your big words,
withdraw, become
so small, so close
to your chest,
that soon
they are points
you never even made.

Riddle

My head is composed of many lobes and desires:
one clove does math,
another remembers how you laugh.
I can be cloven, cleft
in two, then left again.

In French, I am *en chemise*.
In English, I have skin
and am minced. I wish
I'd been French
and simply undressed.

Relic

Let me put you in perspective:
You are far away and small. I am here and big.
I am an entourage of one for what's left
of Cavallini's fresco of Jesus' beltway of angels.
My mother will be happy to know the face of the angel
with the sour expression has been lost.
I recognize the wave an angel gives another angel
as the wave one gives in the country.
Another angel crosses her wings like a lady angel.
As frequently happens, only god has a halo handler.
As frequently happens, the façade
was bigger than the church like eyes
which are bigger than stomachs.
As frequently happens, the church
was never built but the relics
were nonrefundable so I put them
in my cryptoporticus and then abruptly
closed it to the public. I'm sorry
if I got overly thorough on you just now.
As frequently happens, the thing to do
is almost always overly emotionally charged.
Like when I built my own relic
from my own head with the tiny and dull scissors
of a travel sewing kit and I gave it to you
to keep forever and ever and ever and ever
or else I threw it in the hotel's bathroom trash
to keep until the maid came.

The Muses Narrate a Slideshow

History

Here I am sucking on cherry pits
leftover from the cult of Mithras.

Dance

Here I am on a child's sarcophagus:
children collecting walnuts to chuck
at a pyramid of walnuts.

Comedy

Here I am with my melon hairstyle
and my prosciutto smile which identify me
as belonging to the 2nd century.

Music

Here I am the sound of one sense
through a bone flute in past tense.

Hymns

Here I am as she who walks and as she
who walks behind and as she who walks behind behind
and is only a hand which pours water or wine.

Astronomy

Here I am as a pair of sheet bronze hands
with gold buttons to navigate by.

Epic Poetry

Here I am writing epic poetry in my head
since I lost my epic pen.

Love

Here I am announcing the flood.

Tragedy

Here I am a copy of a copy
of an original feeling now lost.

Self-Portrait as the Sound of San Carlito

We say *in sum* to summon some kind
of meaning. When we don't know what

to say we say *um*. The instruments
of my discipline are hunger, ink,

a martyr's thimble wrapped in pink.
Wonder drives us if we're lucky.

I'll follow any crumb anywhere
just to be un-numbed. High July—

the humidity is a kind of drumbeat
on the dumb body. Sometimes a place

looks good enough to plunder.
Sometimes a husband says come home

sometime he won't. But I wouldn't want
such summons. Not that I know what I want:

I'm a statue who's lost her original thought,
a metal stamp with a clichéd *i* to dot.

Venison

Here the deer
are so tame
they come closer
than back in my real life.
Walking down the dirt road
a deer walks beside me
in the field. *A good shot,*
I think, gun
in head.

*

I wrote that a year ago
that was years ago.
Now it looks
like a metaphor.
Like: *what I wanted*
came closer then. Like:
my desire is stuffed
and mounted on my walls.
Like: *it looks at me*
with glass eyes.

Once, *venison* meant
any animal hunted,
meant *whatever was wanted.*
Once, whatever I had
a shot at, I shot at.

And it looks like this
is what that
was about.

Hocus Focus

Find the differences
between the two panels.

Arm is moved
Hat is different
Leaf is missing
Foot is moved
Skirt is longer
Sleeve is shorter
Summer is shorter
Temper is shorter
Something is different
Heart on sleeve is missing
Heart fell off shorter sleeve
Chest is different
Chest is emptier
Smile is smaller
Hand is missing
John is Joe
Hot is colder
Time is longer
Life is shorter
Young is older
You are missing
You are moved
I am not
Everything is different

"…How Delightful it Might Be if None of Them Should Come Out Again"

—Henry James, Capri and the Bay of Naples

After Pompeii
        —and its concrete response,
the body's death cast back;
after the dog straining the chain,
crushing its own windpipe;
after the man, hands up;
after the woman hiding her eyes
from heat's reproach—

you'll want to catch a catamaran to Capri,
get a room, and set up shop by the pool
where the grappa will string you on as long
as you let it. Evenings, you'll unreel

down the island's dark roads singing
all sorts of *auld lang synes*, refrain
from nothing, slip into seaside discos
where the bass drowns out—out-drowns—the sea,
where a lighthouse righthooks the night.
It sees stars as do you.

At daybreak you'll throw yourself
to the Blue Grotto, thread the cave's eye,
swim in its light translation, the sky
roped in.

You'll think fondly of dying here—no accusation
of ash, no cast of you to speak of
you. You
will float on your back—at last

let off the leash
in the bleach of this blue solution, in light

of this hard heaven overhead

San Clemente

I descended to the 4th century
by the route they had marked.

There was a life under this one,
and another under that. It was like

going back in time except I wasn't
any better or purer,

and no matter the life I was under
surveillance. No, I hadn't been aware

that Jesus came from an almond. No,
I hadn't known of the annual miracle

involving withdrawal
and an underwater tomb. It was all

very *Raiders of the Lost Ark*.
Annually, I do the opposite of withdraw

and that is my miracle. *Here is where
the flood rose to,* said the tour guide.

There was no air where you are standing.
But there was no guide.

It was up to me to take myself down
a notch or two. Ascending to the present,

there was a bust in the ticket area
of some Caesar for sale, and behind the bust

a mirror in which I fixed my hair.
I'm so over myself.

Modern Aubade

I lived a lifetime of aubades
sitting for twenty minutes in the exhibit

of the emperor's wife's sunken,
garden room, a light-show simulating day

on fast-forward and repeat. Every two minutes,
the lights would dawn on me,

blow past lunch and then conjure up
a sinking feeling that another day had passed

with nothing to show for it. All this to show
how the room would have looked in the light

it never would have seen. I admit,
it was cool there, a good place to sleep,

or eat, or make that love we kept meaning
to make. That reminds me: I never wrote

that aubade for you, did I? Every sunset,
the quince looked ready. If only

I were a little more chimerical—half-woman,
half-myth—I would have stepped over

the trompe l'oeil wicker fence
and picked them to my heart's content.

Acknowledgements

I would like to thank the editors of the following journals, where some of these poems first appeared, some with different titles or in slightly different forms.

AGNI: "Self-Portrait as Porcupine"
Cincinnatti Review: "Pie Hole," "Shelley's Jaw"
Crazyhorse: "Descent," "A Vestal Virgin Holds Her Breath, Counts to Ten"
The Florida Review: "Rus in Urbe"
The Laurel Review: "Grenade," "Honeymoon"
Mare Nostrum: "Daphne in *As the World Turns*," "Misunderstanding"
Monarch Review: "Modern Aubade," "The Muses Narrate A Slideshow," "This Myth," "Self-Storage"
Poetry: "Another Plot Cliché," "Heart, My Box of Snow," "What For?
Poetry Northwest: "Come Here," "Lion's Teeth," "Song from the Antarctic," "Woodwinds"
POOL: "L'Oeuf," "Suck"
Review: "The Short List"
Smartish Pace: "Pseudomorph," "Self-Portrait as the Sound of San Carlito"
The Southeast Review: "Miss Scarlet"

"Commute" and "Honeymoon" appeared in Alive at the Center: An Anthology of Poems from the Pacific Northwest (Ooligan Press, 2013).

"Lion's Teeth" also appeared in *Poetry Daily: Poems from the World's Most Popular Website* (Sourcebooks Trade, 2003).

Some of these poems previously appeared in a chapbook, *Grenade* (Green-Tower Press, 2005).

I am grateful to the MacDowell Colony, Artist Trust of Washington State, Jack Straw Productions, The Helen Riaboff Whiteley Center at the University of Washington's Friday Harbor Laboratories, and the University of Washington's Rome Center for their generous support.

I am so grateful to so many who are a part of this book.

Thank you to my teachers: Richard Kenney, Linda Bierds, Heather McHugh, Ira Sadoff, and Peter Harris.
Thank you to Robert Hahn, my MacDowell Virgil.

Thank you to Linda Bowers and all of my colleagues at Seattle Arts & Lectures for their support all of those summers when I decamped for Rome.

Thank you to my dear friends and writing group members for sustaining me over the decade of this book's making: Sierra Nelson, Catherine Wing, Cody Walker, Dana Elkun, Ariana Kelly, Julie Larios, Jason Whitmarsh, Kevin Craft, Johnny Horton, Erin Malone, Kary Wayson, and Martha Silano.

And thank you especially to my family: Mom & Dad; Gram & Gramps; Nathan, Liz, Aiden, and Jane Eliza; Elizabeth; Mer; and, of course, to Lar.

CPSIA information can be obtained at www.ICGtesting.com
Printed in the USA
LVOW130510130613

338387LV00002B/4/P

9 781622 880157